C000138211

McINTYRE HOUSE

For support of McIntyre House
we offer our deepest gratitude to:
James K.M. Cheng
Gilic Developments
David McIntyre & Yvonne Chang
Gregory Borowski
Merrick Architecture

For support of the West Coast Modern House
series, we acknowledge the generosity of:
Terry Lyons, Julie Paul and Whitney Lyons
Keith Hemphill of Rositch Hemphill Architects
Bryce Rositch of Rositch Hemphill Architects
Christopher Foundation

ORO Editions
Publishers of Architecture, Art, and Design
Gordon Goff, publisher
www.oroeditions.com
info@oroeditions.com

ISBN 978-1-943532-94-0

10 9 8 7 6 5 4 3 2 1   FIRST EDITION

Text by Sherry McKay
Preface by Douglas Coupland
Photographs by Michael Perlmutter
Drawings by Lõrinc Vass
Series Curation by Leslie Van Duzer, Sherry McKay, and Christopher Macdonald

Book design by Pablo Mandel
www.circularstudio.com

This book has been typeset in Akzidenz Grotesk.

Color Separations and Printing: ORO Group Ltd.
Printed in China

Library of Congress data available upon request. World Rights: Available
International Distribution: www.oroeditions.com/distribution

Photographs by Michael Perlmutter unless otherwise noted.

McINTYRE HOUSE

SHERRY McKAY

PREFACE BY DOUGLAS COUPLAND

PHOTOGRAPHY BY MICHAEL PERLMUTTER

UBC SALA | WEST COAST MODERN HOUSE SERIES

CONTENTS

Editor's Note

With this eighth and final volume, we bring the UBC SALA West Coast Modern House series to a close. Collectively, the houses featured represent the rich diversity of our local modernist tradition, a heritage now seriously imperiled by Vancouver's rapidly escalating land values. The aim of this project was to ensure a thorough documentation of significant works (albeit a limited collection), and if the gods were smiling, perhaps at critical junctures, to save some from demolition.

In the case of the Friedman House by Frederic Lasserre, news of the book reached a distant, sympathetic homebuyer and the house was saved, thanks to the initiative of author Richard Cavell and journalist Kerry Gold, the support of Friedman House's landscape architect Cornelia Hahn Oberlander and the generosity of realtor Evan Ho. Thankfully, three other houses are currently in the caring hands of their original occupants (Downs II, Smith II and McIntyre) and two more have owners well aware of their treasures (Merrick and Binning). Copp House is sited precariously on a highly valued property not far from UBC, while the charming and enigmatic Shumiatcher House is already just a memory.

It took a village to create this series; there are so many people to thank. First, heartfelt thanks to my SALA colleagues and co-editors, Sherry McKay and Chris Macdonald, for bringing their expertise on local West Coast modernism to this project through the series' curation, manuscript editing and the monographs they authored. Their deep knowledge of our region's architectural heritage was invaluable for the success of this project. To all the authors who contributed, thank you for your enthusiastic embrace of your subjects and for the copious amount of time and talent you contributed. It was a great pleasure and honour to work with you. To all the homeowners who granted (and regranted) the authors and photographer generous access, thank you. Your historical documents, intimate stories and family photos all greatly enriched the histories told.

Photographer Michael Perlmutter made numerous trips from his home in Stockholm to participate in this project. His fresh perspective and keen eye afforded us exquisite photographs, an essential component of each volume, a major part of each story. For every book, new drawings, often requiring laborious on-site documentation, were created by SALA students or alumni: Tyler Brown, Justin Neenan and Lőrinc Vass. Pablo Mandel of Circular Studio, graphic designer of the series, gifted us his exceptional talent, and his easy-going manner smoothed the entire production process. Pablo introduced us to Gordon Goff of ORO Editions, who in turn offered us his early trust and two exceptional and indispensable editors: Ryan Buresh and Jake Anderson.

A huge debt of gratitude is owed to the Canada Council for the Arts for supporting two of the volumes (Downs II and Binning) and to the many individuals and businesses who generously contributed to making the other six possible. Among those are Nancy and Niels Bendtsen, owners of Inform Interiors, who have additionally opened their doors and graciously hosted, together with their wonderful staff, all our book launches. Finally, thank you to Ron Kellett, Director of SALA, for the school's ongoing support of this project.

To close, we remember the late Joe Wei who encouraged us to be more active in documenting and preserving our endangered local heritage. This series is dedicated to his memory.

— Leslie Van Duzer

Preface

I remember my first visit to Scott and Corky McIntyre's house. It was a (yes) dark and rainy night and I'd just driven up the North Vancouver's Delbrook Avenue from the Trans-Canada. The Delbrook neighborhood was developed in the late 1950s and early 1960s, and it remains a hillside museum of CMHC housing with many post-and-beams thrown in. I just assumed their place would also be similarly cookie cutter, when about half a kilometer up the hill I turned off onto Cartelier Road and then onto Cartelier Place and...my brain basically exploded. I wasn't expecting what I found: a West Coast rainforest into which five astonishing cedar-clad houses were, even in the dark, obviously elegantly situated. No lawns. No curbs. Forest all around. I then knocked on the door and when Corky opened it, I walked into what can honestly be called, for me, a version of heaven.

I came of age in the 1970s and am, in good and bad ways, a product of the era. There was night skiing several nights a week on Grouse Mountain, and everyone got a used car at sixteen. Vancouver was also the home of Greenpeace, and I was the first wave of young people who had been ecologically informed from kindergarten on up. This was training that engendered in most people like me a deep cynicism about large planned systems: big governments, big corporations—or basically anything overly organized. So, to enter the McIntyre's house was to enter a solution to the problems of the world. It is constructed using raw cedar, and exposed beams, and when lit with incandescent bulbs, it seemingly glowed from within. Its spaces were covered with simple rustic and handmade carpeting, except for the living room into which was nested flokati carpeting in front of a big-ass concrete fireplace. The artwork on the walls was both genuine and totally of the era. And perhaps best of all, when it's raining outside, which is a lot of the time, one senses the rain and is one with it, at peace with it, as it patters on the cedar shingle roof.

I mentioned skiing earlier. In the very early pre-corporate days of Whistler, ski cabins similar to McIntyre House were built in much the same way. Their aesthetic derived from being on steep unusual sites, which often led to the structures using 45-degree angles to connect one floor to another. The cedar planks and bands on the walls acted like supergraphics, a form of graphic treatment that came and went with the 1970s. These ski cabins were also built on budgets and had to handle weather extremes not experienced in Vancouver. Pretty much all of this defines McIntyre House, but it doesn't factor in the personalities of Scott and Corky. Scott, a publisher, squeezed the books he published into every available crack in the walls. Corky, who comes from a prairie family, brought a minimal prairie sweetness with her textiles and artefacts. I can imagine there was more than one heated discussion over whether a nook should be filled with fifty books or a single vase containing a single wildflower.

The house is also a house for all seasons. Spring and fall are rainy seasons when the house almost becomes a living creature keeping one warm and protected. In summer the house transforms as sunlight cuts through and above the hundred-foot-tall hemlocks and firs, illuminating the vine maples below like stained glass, as birdsong fills the air above the creek below, a zoological freeway for larger mammals such as bears, deer, coyotes and raccoons. The summer sunlight at the end of the afternoon, makes airborne seeds glow, and makes you feel as if everything around you is just as alive as you are—which is actually true. And then there is winter, and winter means the fireplace, definitely the heart of the house, where Scott and Corky read books in heated bliss while the outside world hibernates. It doesn't get cozier than this.

I miss that people once built houses like McIntyre House, homes that so elegantly address the time and place they live in, and which cost no more to build than ugly houses. Why are there no more than a few of these houses in existence? I suppose that is the magic of the place, that it was built in the first place, and that it has survived, and that it shows us there was once a different, and yes, better way to live life in Vancouver.

— Douglas Coupland

Acknowledgements

I would particularly like to thank the McIntyres for welcoming me into their home and sharing memories and documentation of both house and landscape. They are the inspiration for my narrative of the house. Barry Griblin graciously provided images and published material pertinent to Cartelier Place for which I am greatly appreciative. I am especially grateful to James Cheng who astutely identified McIntyre House as a hidden gem of West Coast modern architecture and substantially sponsored the project.

There are many individuals who have contributed to the production of this publication. I am indebted to SALA alumnus Lőrinc Vass for his superb drawings, Stockholm-based Michael Perlmutter for capturing in photographs the magic of the house and landscape, and Pablo Mandel in Buenos Aires for his astute graphic skills.

Finally, I would like to recognize the commitment of Leslie Van Duzer to the SALA West Coast Modern House series and her support as editor and colleague in the writing of McIntyre House.

— Sherry McKay

McIntyre House complies with the logic of the temperate rainforest, stretching upward to catch the light and spreading out to the opportunities offered at the forest floor. More than metaphor, this comparison calls attention to McIntrye House as an eloquent proposition for how one might reside within sensitive eco-systems.

Beginning

McIntyre House perches on a remnant of a temperate coastal forest on the southern slope of the North Shore Mountains. When the developer, Lois Milsom, originally paced the site, before the construction of the house and the cul-de-sac on which it sits, Cartelier Place, she saw not only a residual forest, but also envisioned an innovative modern architecture harmoniously residing within it. Indeed, the forest would become a culturally imbued landscape.

The house that finally resulted in 1973 is redolent of the myth of a particular West Coast idiom: timber structures weathered by the elements and time; integrated interior and exterior spaces via the decks and patios permitted by a benign climate; agile forms adaptive to topography and receptive to vegetation, rain and elusive sunlight. The house is nurtured by a modernist architectural sensibility that eschewed convention to create pragmatic, complex volumes attuned to the temporal dimension of spatial experience. While abstract in form and practical in conception, the house is also permeated with an aesthetic of the local, an architecture commensurate with concurrent artistic innovations: Bill Reid's mythical references to place conveyed via abstract form and Jack Shadbolt's celebration of the forest floor with carefully framed views of its offerings.

A photograph of Lois Milsom at the site prior to its development shows her standing in shafts of sunlight filtered through tall conifers, in the midst of stumps, fallen boughs and scattered ferns. The sense of untrammelled nature experienced in this initial encounter would determine many design features of the development, not least of which was the expensive subterranean service infrastructure.[1] Cartelier Place would become the site of an inventive proposition for topographically attuned suburban living amidst, and in contra-distinction to, neighbouring conventional streets and customary lots.[2] It was initially conceived by Milsom and Hassell / Griblin, of Comprehensive Architectural Services, Ltd., as a "Strata Garden Development" in 1968. Together, the developer and designers proposed a compact cluster of townhouses, enabled by recent legislation allowing strata ownership.[3] By 1970, after resistance from neighbouring property owners, the strata-titled townhouses were abandoned and Cartelier Place became seven single-family homes judiciously placed within the 3½-acre site. Each plot was sized and configured according to the topography, with minimized tree loss and sensitivity to two fish-bearing creeks that followed the slope of the site. This unorthodox approach to the site, which eliminated standardized setbacks and side yards of conventional subdivisions, was a result of independent zoning conferred on the development.[4] While each house varies according to the particularities of its site, the five designed and built by Hassell / Griblin share a formal vocabulary consequent of vertically extruded volumes raised on minimal footings and canted to capture light.

Robert Hassell and Barry Griblin graduated from UBC School of Architecture in the mid-1960s, and extended the idealism engendered there to a design/build practice that fostered an intimate dialogue with the landscape and future occupants.[5] These designer/builders merged a high modernist preoccupation with space, "of working in the 3rd and 4th dimension," with an economy-minded construction savvy that produced simple, inexpensive shells of systematized proportions and typified details.[6] While both roof and foundations were minimized in the interest of economy, the relatively inexpensive and flexible timber frame could extrude canted bays, extend with shed roofs, and retract into skylights to opportunely capture the sun or avoid a neighbour's overlook. The timber frame in such vertically arrayed terrain invited a reorganizing of program in section: entrances positioned at mid-level adjacent to public spaces with private spaces above and below. These concepts are evident in all five houses they built for Cartelier Place.[7] While each house shared in these design principles and strategies, each was particularized according to client desires and terrain.[8]

In 1970, Scott and Corky McIntyre had just returned to the West Coast from Toronto, Scott to eventually embark on a publishing venture that would become Douglas & McIntyre, Corky to continue a career as a librarian. In the summer of 1971 they accidently came across Cartelier Place. The McIntyres were enamoured by its woods and streams and its show home that bewitched with its improbable capture of light, unanticipated spaces and wood-clad forms that seemed so apt in its forested, creek-side setting. It also seemed unaffordable. Revisiting the site in early 1972, the anticipation of their first child now giving some urgency to their quest for a home, they found several lots still available.

After pursing the possibility of living there, they negotiated the purchase of the 9,800 square foot "lot b" from Lois Milsom for $19,000. Robert Hassell of Hassell / Griblin was contracted to design, and, with builder John LeFevre, construct what would become an approximately 1,500 square foot timber-and-glass house, for an affordable $20.00 a square foot. The McIntyres were one of the first to purchase a lot in Cartelier Place, to commission a house and, in October 1973, to move in.[9] They continue to live there some 45 years later.

The original design of the McIntyre home was informed by the overall progressive proposition of Cartelier Place: affordability won by a post-and-beam structure on minimal point supports; spatial ingenuity that distributed private spaces from centrally located public areas; and a feeling of spaciousness rather than abundant square footage. Siting and orientation ensured privacy from overlook. These design commitments were brought to bear on the specificities of the McIntyre program: two bedrooms, one with a playroom, the other with a study, both with adjacent bathrooms; a living room with fireplace, a kitchen equipped with washer and dryer, augmented with a family eating area and formal dining room, wide halls and linen closets—and a library.

A forest can elicit dreams of cabin retreats and tree forts. A creek invites their location nearby. The forest and creek of the McIntyre House property conjured such a library retreat in the woods, withdrawn from the house, beyond the creek, across a bridge. It would be an appropriate reverie for the future residents, one a publisher of books, the other a librarian. Alas, in the end, the library was left to the imagination rather than disturb or destabilize the creek with foundations of the required bridge. However, other imaginings were fulfilled, each alteration to the house invited by the possibilities inherent in the existing structure. In 1980 a deck was enlarged to the south and the front entrance sequence altered; in 2007, the kitchen was expanded and a bathroom on the main level inserted.

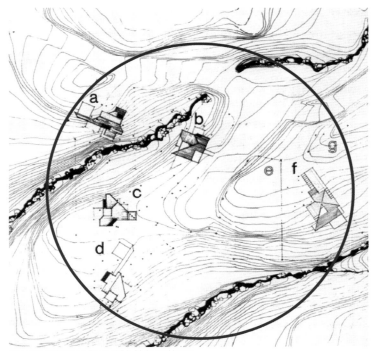

Site Plan of Cartelier Place, "b" is McIntyre House
Hassell / Griblin. Courtesy of Barry Griblin

Photographs: Corky McIntyre. Courtesy of Scott and Corky McIntyre

Photograph: Hassell / Griblin. Courtesy of Barry Griblin

Creation

Today, McIntyre House has taken on the hue and texture of the forest. Its austere façade has weathered and the forest has grown around it. Initially, it might appear to be a simple wooden box with a familiar gabled façade to the street, as convention would assume. However, on closer inspection peculiarities are discovered. Seemingly snug against the street, the house is also distanced from it by an intervening chasm into which the east façade descends beneath the ground plane suggested by the entrance, road and adjacent trees. The axis of the roof slope is eccentric, stretched to the south, truncated to the north. A glazed fissure floats off-centre and un-grounded near the roofline. Hidden from view is the slope of the land as it falls away to the west, each of the five half-levels of the house touching the site uniquely; grounded to the east, elevated on point supports to the west, closed to east and north, open to south and west. The interior is an epiphany.

Within, the asceticism of the exterior is transformed by vertiginous views across shafts of space and precarious perches from which treetops become close and flowing water can be heard. Immediately beyond the threshold, an entrance "greenhouse" offers a cascade of southern skylight and, from the north, subtle light filters down from the cleft of glass that so beguiled on the façade. We have entered the house at mid-level and space spins centrifugally from a core of solid chimney and open stair, parsed into five half-levels and finally released into the forest beyond via judiciously placed windows, skylights and glass doors.[10] Space dilates to the double height of the living room, slips below to the kitchen, flows upward to a balconied study and is compressed beneath a mezzanine. The gap between the living room floor and the fall of the land serendipitously suggested a "basement," a boon of storage space and an eventual wine cellar. The double height of the living room invited a focal point for its dramatic rise from floor to rafters; the aggregate, wood-burning fireplace creates a microclimate within the inglenook that it defines, augmenting the house's more conventional central heating. This interior space is dynamic and centrifugal, enlivened by glimpses of elsewhere, the diurnal path of the sun or the seasonal changes of foliage. The interior is strangely light-filled in contrast to the forest-enveloped road that leads to McIntyre House.

While conifers soar above, accompanied by shafts of light and glimpses of blue, the house frames more intimate, detailed portraits: highly textured bark and branches of cedar; the changing colour of flat-leaved vine maples; and the lacey green of ferns, salal and Oregon grape.[11] It is not the distant view and the reassurance of the horizon that the house offers, but rather the delight of the detail and the comfort of enclosure; it is not the singular expanse of the sublime, but the episodic of the picturesque. The house encourages an embrace of the irregularities of the land. It is a reception enhanced by the framing devices of a bench, step, deck or window. These architectural devices focus appreciation on the foliage of trees, the berries of plants or the mossy accoutrements of a nearby creek, the immediate, proximate landscape.

McIntyre House also cultivates a cultural landscape. The autochthonic materials of the house curate a collection of artworks that bestow upon it and its surroundings a cultural resonance. There are paintings and prints by Gordon Smith, Jack Shadbolt and Robert Davidson among others, all artists who have expressed the coastal bearings of their interests. The oneiric library in the woods is still there. It is lurking within the house's walls of masterfully matched, straight-grained, first-growth red cedar shown to dramatic effect in over-height walls, beams that soar overhead and oak floors that provide a comfortable ground underfoot. The presence of books, distributed throughout, many of them Douglas & McIntyre imprints, many exemplified in the artwork, invoke lives lived within the house, a human temporal dimension inserted into the seeming eternity of the forest.

Lois Milson on site. Photograph: Bill Reid. Courtesy of Lois Milsom and Scott and Corky McIntyre

Legacy

The celebration of the house's vertical dimension is a revelation. The innovative exploitation of the building section liberates the potential of stacking small spaces, providing opportunities in their misalignment for volumes that extend over two storeys or compress to form an alcove. The conventional horizontal relationship of house to land is jettisoned to allow a perpendicularity commensurate with the steepness of the incline. While earlier West Coast modern architecture accommodated the uneven terrain of difficult craggy sites, it was invariably with an eye to restoring the comforting horizon and its tendency to the distant view. The vertical of the section liberated in McIntyre House offered new possibilities of nearness to the land and the forest canopy.

The architects proposed "a house in a subdivision that could preserve the natural landscape," where "the design of individual dwellings can complement the setting" and "municipal regulations can be tailored to specific sites."[12] The attention to the form and fall of the land, the damp of the winter forest and its filtered summer warmth in buildings of sympathetic design and compatible materials was not a parochial aspiration. Nor was the focus on the subdivision as a site of relevant, vanguard practice an idiosyncrasy. McIntyre House was, as part of Cartelier Place, part of a larger shift in design sensibilities and approaches to peri-urban development in the mid-1960s. It was a localized exploration comparable to the contemporary Sea Ranch, north of San Francisco.[13] Here too simple wood structures disciplined by precise aesthetic precepts were fashioned from local materials and informed by the ecology of its coastal site. Sea Ranch's initial Condominium One grouped modest dwellings in a single wind-shaped form oriented to capture the ocean views. Cartelier Place—although smaller in scale, less restricted by design guidelines, and engaged with different environmental issues—like Sea Ranch, tested the relationship between profitable real estate development and architecture as a form of land stewardship. These architectural innovations offered alternatives to the template replication of most subdivisions of the preceding decades, seeking affordability in design ingenuity rather than reduced square footage or the economies of mass production.

Both attempted, in the parlance of the day, to turn our attention to "the spirit of the place" and aimed to "touch the land lightly."

McIntyre House is an architecture at home with the damp and the dark, with forest debris and the spongy invasions of fungi and moss. It accommodates the waywardness of a free-flowing water course and celebrates its acoustical offering. It also accepts the herons and racoons as well as the owls and deer that its site attracts. The house is an embrace of the commonly uncelebrated and often excluded forces of nature.[14] Deferential to the creek, respectful of topography and conserving of trees, McIntyre House offered an attentiveness to the ecological aspects of architecture's engagement with the environment before legislation and professional bodies recognized the importance of such considerations.

If McIntyre House were a book, it would be a quiet manifesto, one aiming to reframe the processes of architecture and construction through the prism of the environment and its sustainability. And like a book, McIntyre House offers a story of the West Coast crafted by many talents (builder, publisher, librarian and various muses). The house creates an impression of life in a forest, and, like a memory, is something that you can take away with you.

Photographs: Corky McIntyre. Courtesy of Scott and Corky McIntyre

Notes

1. Lois Milsom as developer absorbed the significant costs entailed in burying the services. Conversations with Scott McIntyre (August 2019).
2. Initially Milsom, working with Hassell / Griblin, proposed townhouses for the site. However, there was opposition from neighboring properties that either wanted a more conventional road access and housing type, or wanted no development at all so as to leave the property as part of the park system of the area. Barry Griblin, "Cartelier Road Development / Strata Garden Development 1968/9," a conversation with Lois Milsom (conversation 18 April 2019, text written by Griblin 23 April 2019), Scott McIntyre personal files, North Vancouver.
3. Griblin, "Cartelier Road Development."
4. According to Barry Griblin, the original Strata Garden Development zoning was based on a contractual agreement with the District of North Vancouver. It was a variation of the District of North Vancouver Garden Apartment Zone zoning. Griblin, "Cartelier Road Development."
5. UBC School of Architecture archives records Griblin graduating in 1965 and Hassell in 1967.
6. Hassell quoted in Robert Gretton, "Projects by Hassell / Griblin, Vancouver," *The Canadian Architect* (April 1974): 27.
7. Hassell quoted in Gretton, 27.
8. Barry Griblin, Notes on Cartelier Road Development, Scott McIntyre personal files, North Vancouver.
9. In fact, the McIntyres may have been the first to actually commission a house in the Cartelier Place development. According to Barry Griblin, "the first lot sold in the new subdivision was to Scott and Corky McIntyre." Griblin, "Cartelier Road Development." By 1974, of the three houses that had been built, two had been speculative and only one, the McIntyre's, had been commissioned specifically. Gretton, 29.
10. Originally, one entered into a perfunctory entrance that had immediately to the left (south) a closet and directly to the right (north) a stair down to the eating area and kitchen. The entrance was enlarged by enclosing the deck that initially fronted the southeast corner of the façade.
11. Don Vaughn, planting design site plan, 1979. Note existing vine maples and fir, a hemlock removed and the annotation: "native material as existing." Indigenous plants were carefully cultivated and augmented with other native plants: azeleas, rhododendrons, pieris and sumac.
12. Griblin, Notes.
13. Sea Ranch was first designed in 1965 but was not developed until 1968. Cartelier Place was first proposed as a townhouse strata title development in 1968/9. See Donlyn Lyndon and James Alinder, *The Sea Ranch: 50 Years of Architecture, Landscape, Place and Community on the Northern California Coast*, 2nd Edition (New York: Princeton Architectural Press, 2014).
14. In the new millennium, these aspects of nature have become a source of architectural inventiveness and a response to current environmental concerns. See David Gissen, *Subnature: Architecture's Other Environments* (New York: Princeton Architectural Press, 2009).

PHOTOGRAPHS

DRAWINGS

Site Plan

1. North Deck (not completed)
2. Main Entry Deck (subsequently partially enclosed)
3. Living Room Deck (shown in current enlarged state)

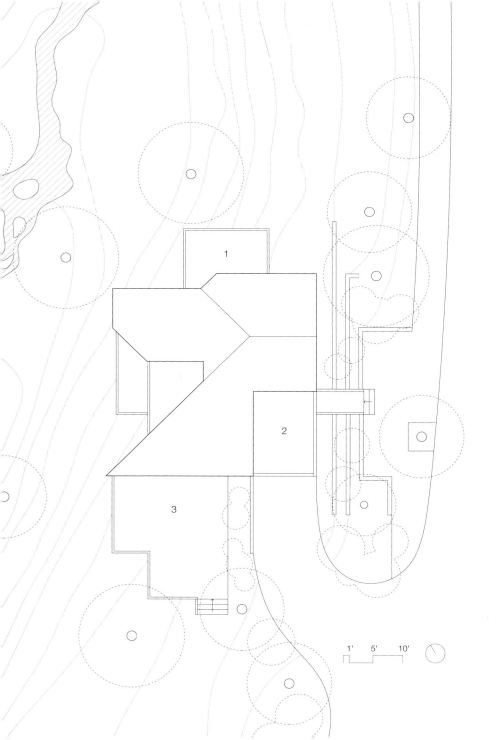

1

2

3

1'   5'   10'

South Elevation

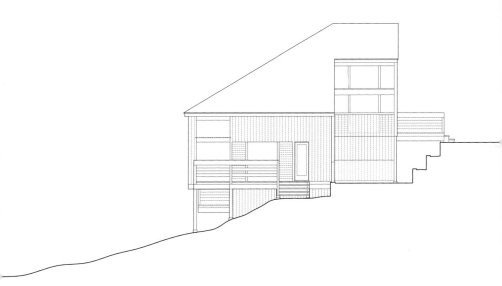

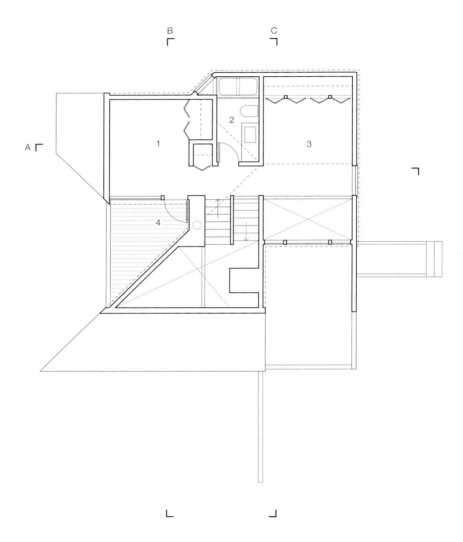

1. Bedroom
2. Bathroom
3. Study
4. Deck

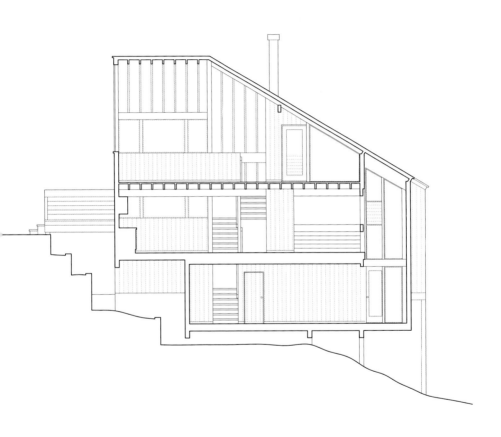

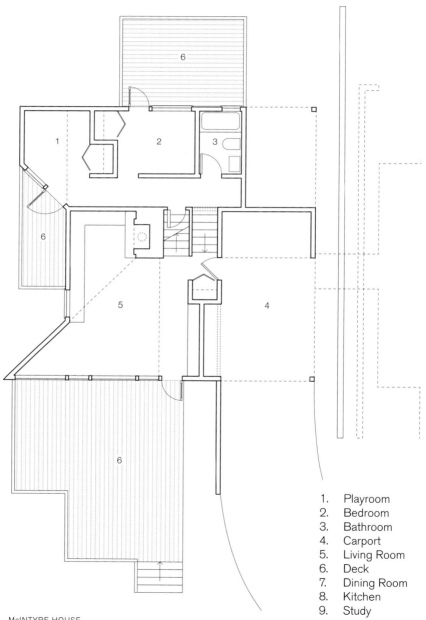

1. Playroom
2. Bedroom
3. Bathroom
4. Carport
5. Living Room
6. Deck
7. Dining Room
8. Kitchen
9. Study

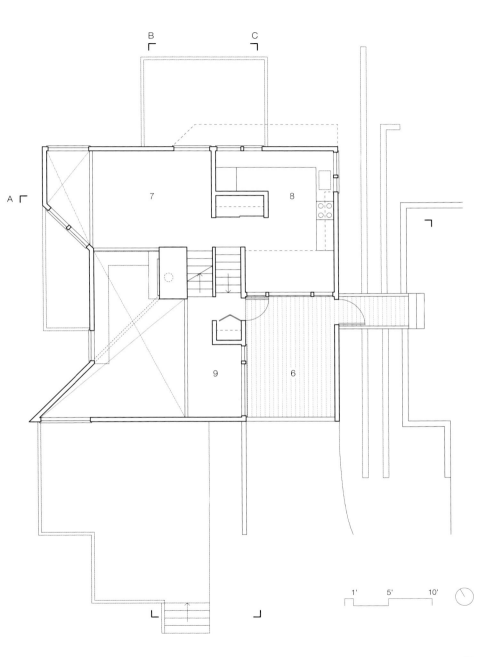

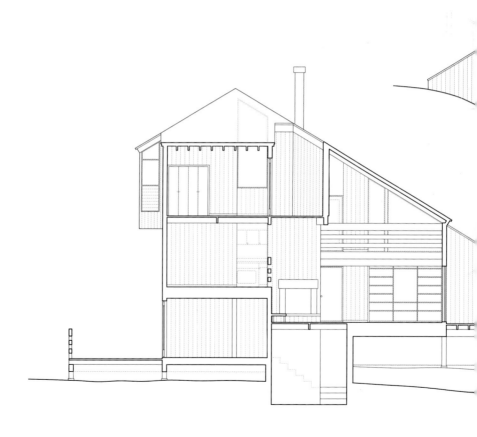

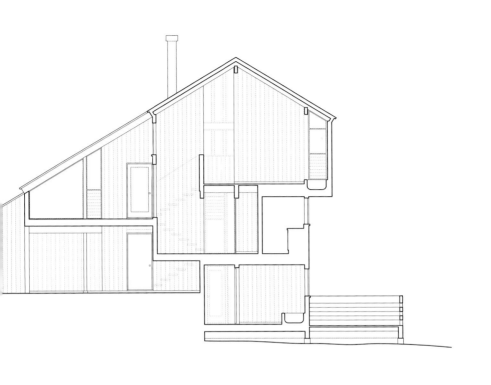

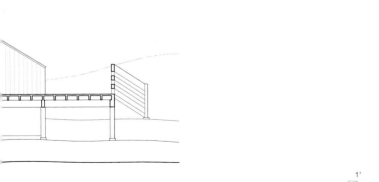

1' 5' 10'

West and North Elevations

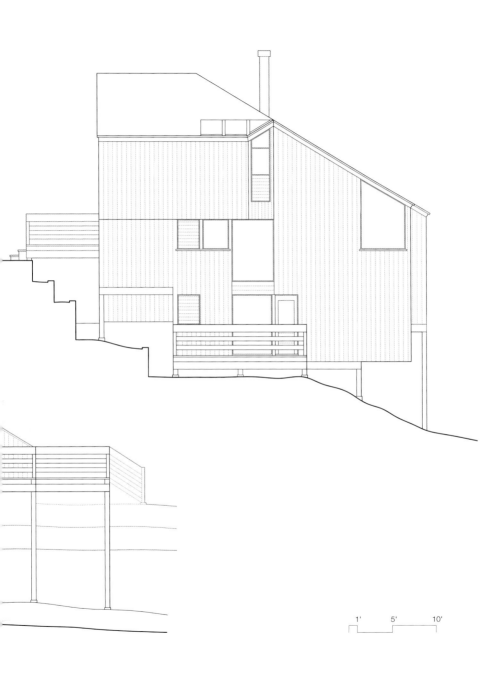

1'   5'   10'

Series
UBC SALA West Coast Modern House

House Shumiatcher
Leslie Van Duzer

Downs House II
Christopher Macdonald

Merrick House
Anthony Robins

Binning House
Matthew Soules

Friedman House
Richard Cavell

Copp House
Adele Weder

Smith House II
Michael Prokopow with Douglas Coupland

McIntyre House
Sherry McKay with Douglas Coupland

Credits

Sherry McKay Author, Series Editor

Sherry McKay is an architectural historian and as of 2019 Professor Emerita of the UBC School of Architecture and Landscape (SALA). She was the recipient of a Killam Teaching Award and inaugural Chair of the architecture program in SALA (2006-09). Her work on West Coast architecture and French architecture of the modern colonial era appears in North American and French publications. She has contributed essays to exhibition catalogues of the Vancouver Art Gallery, Museum of Vancouver and the Contemporary Art Gallery (Vancouver). She was exhibition organizer and catalogue author for *Assembling Utopia: packaging the home,* at the Canadian Embassy in Tokyo in 2000. From 2010 to 2017 she was the Book Review Editor of the UK journal *Building Research and Information.* Recently published is her "West Coast Land Claims," *Canadian Modern Architecture,* 1967 to the present (Princeton Architectural Press, 2019). Currently she is exploring the notion of "building fictions," history told via the material vicissitudes and appropriations of architecture.

Douglas Coupland Preface

Since 1991 Coupland has written thirteen novels published in most languages. He has written and performed for England's Royal Shakespeare Company. He is a columnist for the *Financial Times* of London and frequent contributor to the *New York Times, e-flux, DIS* and *Vice.* In 2000 Coupland amplified his visual art production and has recently had two separate museum retrospectives, "Everything is Anything is Anywhere is Everywhere" and "Bit Rot." Coupland is a member of the Royal Canadian Academy and an Officer of the Order of Canada.

Michael Perlmutter Photographer

After completing his Master of Architecture degree at UC Berkeley, Michael moved to Sweden in 1989, working first as an architect. Five